Syllabus

SUPREME COURT OF THE UNITED STATES

Syllabus

NORTH CAROLINA STATE BOARD OF DENTAL EXAMINERS *v.* FEDERAL TRADE COMMISSION

CERTIORARI TO THE UNITED STATES COURT OF APPEALS FOR THE FOURTH CIRCUIT

No. 13–534.   Argued October 14, 2014—Decided February 25, 2015

North Carolina's Dental Practice Act (Act) provides that the North Carolina State Board of Dental Examiners (Board) is "the agency of the State for the regulation of the practice of dentistry." The Board's principal duty is to create, administer, and enforce a licensing system for dentists; and six of its eight members must be licensed, practicing dentists.

The Act does not specify that teeth whitening is "the practice of dentistry." Nonetheless, after dentists complained to the Board that nondentists were charging lower prices for such services than dentists did, the Board issued at least 47 official cease-and-desist letters to nondentist teeth whitening service providers and product manufacturers, often warning that the unlicensed practice of dentistry is a crime. This and other related Board actions led nondentists to cease offering teeth whitening services in North Carolina.

The Federal Trade Commission (FTC) filed an administrative complaint, alleging that the Board's concerted action to exclude nondentists from the market for teeth whitening services in North Carolina constituted an anticompetitive and unfair method of competition under the Federal Trade Commission Act. An Administrative Law Judge (ALJ) denied the Board's motion to dismiss on the ground of state-action immunity. The FTC sustained that ruling, reasoning that even if the Board had acted pursuant to a clearly articulated state policy to displace competition, the Board must be actively supervised by the State to claim immunity, which it was not. After a hearing on the merits, the ALJ determined that the Board had unreasonably restrained trade in violation of antitrust law. The FTC again sustained the ALJ, and the Fourth Circuit affirmed the FTC in all respects.

Held: Because a controlling number of the Board's decisionmakers are active market participants in the occupation the Board regulates, the Board can invoke state-action antitrust immunity only if it was subject to active supervision by the State, and here that requirement is not met. Pp. 5–18.

(a) Federal antitrust law is a central safeguard for the Nation's free market structures. However, requiring States to conform to the mandates of the Sherman Act at the expense of other values a State may deem fundamental would impose an impermissible burden on the States' power to regulate. Therefore, beginning with *Parker* v. *Brown*, 317 U. S. 341, this Court interpreted the antitrust laws to confer immunity on the anticompetitive conduct of States acting in their sovereign capacity. Pp. 5–6.

(b) The Board's actions are not cloaked with *Parker* immunity. A nonsovereign actor controlled by active market participants—such as the Board—enjoys *Parker* immunity only if " 'the challenged restraint . . . [is] clearly articulated and affirmatively expressed as state policy,' and . . . 'the policy . . . [is] actively supervised by the State.' " *FTC* v. *Phoebe Putney Health System, Inc.*, 568 U. S. ___, ___ (quoting *California Retail Liquor Dealers Assn.* v. *Midcal Aluminum, Inc.*, 445 U. S. 97, 105). Here, the Board did not receive active supervision of its anticompetitive conduct. Pp. 6–17.

(1) An entity may not invoke *Parker* immunity unless its actions are an exercise of the State's sovereign power. See *Columbia* v. *Omni Outdoor Advertising, Inc.*, 499 U. S. 365, 374. Thus, where a State delegates control over a market to a nonsovereign actor the Sherman Act confers immunity only if the State accepts political accountability for the anticompetitive conduct it permits and controls. Limits on state-action immunity are most essential when a State seeks to delegate its regulatory power to active market participants, for dual allegiances are not always apparent to an actor and prohibitions against anticompetitive self-regulation by active market participants are an axiom of federal antitrust policy. Accordingly, *Parker* immunity requires that the anticompetitive conduct of nonsovereign actors, especially those authorized by the State to regulate their own profession, result from procedures that suffice to make it the State's own. *Midcal's* two-part test provides a proper analytical framework to resolve the ultimate question whether an anticompetitive policy is indeed the policy of a State. The first requirement—clear articulation—rarely will achieve that goal by itself, for entities purporting to act under state authority might diverge from the State's considered definition of the public good and engage in private self-dealing. The second *Midcal* requirement—active supervision—seeks to avoid this

harm by requiring the State to review and approve interstitial policies made by the entity claiming immunity. Pp. 6–10.

(2) There are instances in which an actor can be excused from *Midcal*'s active supervision requirement. Municipalities, which are electorally accountable, have general regulatory powers, and have no private price-fixing agenda, are subject exclusively to the clear articulation requirement. See *Hallie* v. *Eau Claire*, 471 U. S. 34, 35. That *Hallie* excused municipalities from *Midcal*'s supervision rule for these reasons, however, all but confirms the rule's applicability to actors controlled by active market participants. Further, in light of *Omni*'s holding that an otherwise immune entity will not lose immunity based on ad hoc and *ex post* questioning of its motives for making particular decisions, 499 U. S., at 374, it is all the more necessary to ensure the conditions for granting immunity are met in the first place, see *FTC* v. *Ticor Title Ins. Co.*, 504 U. S. 621, 633, and *Phoebe Putney*, *supra*, at ___. The clear lesson of precedent is that *Midcal*'s active supervision test is an essential prerequisite of *Parker* immunity for any nonsovereign entity—public or private—controlled by active market participants. Pp. 10–12.

(3) The Board's argument that entities designated by the States as agencies are exempt from *Midcal*'s second requirement cannot be reconciled with the Court's repeated conclusion that the need for supervision turns not on the formal designation given by States to regulators but on the risk that active market participants will pursue private interests in restraining trade. State agencies controlled by active market participants pose the very risk of self-dealing *Midcal*'s supervision requirement was created to address. See *Goldfarb* v. *Virginia State Bar*, 421 U. S. 773, 791. This conclusion does not question the good faith of state officers but rather is an assessment of the structural risk of market participants' confusing their own interests with the State's policy goals. While *Hallie* stated "it is likely that active state supervision would also not be required" for agencies, 471 U. S., at 46, n. 10, the entity there was more like prototypical state agencies, not specialized boards dominated by active market participants. The latter are similar to private trade associations vested by States with regulatory authority, which must satisfy *Midcal*'s active supervision standard. 445 U. S., at 105–106. The similarities between agencies controlled by active market participants and such associations are not eliminated simply because the former are given a formal designation by the State, vested with a measure of government power, and required to follow some procedural rules. See *Hallie*, *supra*, at 39. When a State empowers a group of active market participants to decide who can participate in its market, and on what terms, the need for supervision is manifest. Thus,

the Court holds today that a state board on which a controlling number of decisionmakers are active market participants in the occupation the board regulates must satisfy *Midcal's* active supervision requirement in order to invoke state-action antitrust immunity. Pp. 12–14.

(4) The State argues that allowing this FTC order to stand will discourage dedicated citizens from serving on state agencies that regulate their own occupation. But this holding is not inconsistent with the idea that those who pursue a calling must embrace ethical standards that derive from a duty separate from the dictates of the State. Further, this case does not offer occasion to address the question whether agency officials, including board members, may, under some circumstances, enjoy immunity from damages liability. Of course, States may provide for the defense and indemnification of agency members in the event of litigation, and they can also ensure *Parker* immunity is available by adopting clear policies to displace competition and providing active supervision. Arguments against the wisdom of applying the antitrust laws to professional regulation absent compliance with the prerequisites for invoking *Parker* immunity must be rejected, see *Patrick* v. *Burget*, 486 U. S. 94, 105–106, particularly in light of the risks licensing boards dominated by market participants may pose to the free market. Pp. 14–16.

(5) The Board does not contend in this Court that its anticompetitive conduct was actively supervised by the State or that it should receive *Parker* immunity on that basis. The Act delegates control over the practice of dentistry to the Board, but says nothing about teeth whitening. In acting to expel the dentists' competitors from the market, the Board relied on cease-and-desist letters threatening criminal liability, instead of other powers at its disposal that would have invoked oversight by a politically accountable official. Whether or not the Board exceeded its powers under North Carolina law, there is no evidence of any decision by the State to initiate or concur with the Board's actions against the nondentists. P. 17.

(c) Here, where there are no specific supervisory systems to be reviewed, it suffices to note that the inquiry regarding active supervision is flexible and context-dependent. The question is whether the State's review mechanisms provide "realistic assurance" that a nonsovereign actor's anticompetitive conduct "promotes state policy, rather than merely the party's individual interests." *Patrick*, 486 U. S., 100–101. The Court has identified only a few constant requirements of active supervision: The supervisor must review the substance of the anticompetitive decision, see *id.*, at 102–103; the supervisor must have the power to veto or modify particular decisions to ensure they accord with state policy, see *ibid.*; and the "mere potential for state supervision is not an adequate substitute for a decision by the State," *Ticor, supra*, at 638. Further, the state supervisor may not itself be an active market participant. In general, however, the adequacy of supervision otherwise will depend on all the circumstances of a case. Pp. 17–18.

717 F. 3d 359, affirmed.

KENNEDY, J., delivered the opinion of the Court, in which ROBERTS, C. J., and GINSBURG, BREYER, SOTOMAYOR, and KAGAN, JJ., joined. ALITO, J., filed a dissenting opinion, in which SCALIA and THOMAS, JJ., joined.

SUPREME COURT OF THE UNITED STATES

No. 13–534

NORTH CAROLINA STATE BOARD OF DENTAL EXAMINERS, PETITIONER *v.* FEDERAL TRADE COMMISSION

ON WRIT OF CERTIORARI TO THE UNITED STATES COURT OF APPEALS FOR THE FOURTH CIRCUIT

[February 25, 2015]

JUSTICE KENNEDY delivered the opinion of the Court.

This case arises from an antitrust challenge to the actions of a state regulatory board. A majority of the board's members are engaged in the active practice of the profession it regulates. The question is whether the board's actions are protected from Sherman Act regulation under the doctrine of state-action antitrust immunity, as defined and applied in this Court's decisions beginning with *Parker* v. *Brown*, 317 U. S. 341 (1943).

I

A

In its Dental Practice Act (Act), North Carolina has declared the practice of dentistry to be a matter of public concern requiring regulation. N. C. Gen. Stat. Ann. §90–22(a) (2013). Under the Act, the North Carolina State Board of Dental Examiners (Board) is "the agency of the State for the regulation of the practice of dentistry." §90–22(b).

The Board's principal duty is to create, administer, and enforce a licensing system for dentists. See §§90–29 to

90–41. To perform that function it has broad authority over licensees. See §90–41. The Board's authority with respect to unlicensed persons, however, is more restricted: like "any resident citizen," the Board may file suit to "perpetually enjoin any person from . . . unlawfully practicing dentistry." §90–40.1.

The Act provides that six of the Board's eight members must be licensed dentists engaged in the active practice of dentistry. §90–22. They are elected by other licensed dentists in North Carolina, who cast their ballots in elections conducted by the Board. *Ibid.* The seventh member must be a licensed and practicing dental hygienist, and he or she is elected by other licensed hygienists. *Ibid.* The final member is referred to by the Act as a "consumer" and is appointed by the Governor. *Ibid.* All members serve 3-year terms, and no person may serve more than two consecutive terms. *Ibid.* The Act does not create any mechanism for the removal of an elected member of the Board by a public official. See *ibid.*

Board members swear an oath of office, §138A–22(a), and the Board must comply with the State's Administrative Procedure Act, §150B–1 *et seq.*, Public Records Act, §132–1 *et seq.*, and open-meetings law, §143–318.9 *et seq.* The Board may promulgate rules and regulations governing the practice of dentistry within the State, provided those mandates are not inconsistent with the Act and are approved by the North Carolina Rules Review Commission, whose members are appointed by the state legislature. See §§90–48, 143B–30.1, 150B–21.9(a).

B

In the 1990's, dentists in North Carolina started whitening teeth. Many of those who did so, including 8 of the Board's 10 members during the period at issue in this case, earned substantial fees for that service. By 2003, nondentists arrived on the scene. They charged lower prices for their services than the dentists did. Dentists soon began to complain to the Board about their new competitors. Few complaints warned of possible harm to consumers. Most expressed a principal concern with the low prices charged by nondentists.

Responding to these filings, the Board opened an investigation into nondentist teeth whitening. A dentist member was placed in charge of the inquiry. Neither the Board's hygienist member nor its consumer member participated in this undertaking. The Board's chief operations officer remarked that the Board was "going forth to do battle" with nondentists. App. to Pet. for Cert. 103a. The Board's concern did not result in a formal rule or regulation reviewable by the independent Rules Review Commission, even though the Act does not, by its terms, specify that teeth whitening is "the practice of dentistry."

Starting in 2006, the Board issued at least 47 cease-and-desist letters on its official letterhead to nondentist teeth whitening service providers and product manufacturers. Many of those letters directed the recipient to cease "all activity constituting the practice of dentistry"; warned that the unlicensed practice of dentistry is a crime; and strongly implied (or expressly stated) that teeth whitening constitutes "the practice of dentistry." App. 13, 15. In early 2007, the Board persuaded the North Carolina Board of Cosmetic Art Examiners to warn cosmetologists against providing teeth whitening services. Later that year, the Board sent letters to mall operators, stating that kiosk teeth whiteners were violating the Dental Practice Act and advising that the malls consider expelling violators from their premises.

These actions had the intended result. Nondentists ceased offering teeth whitening services in North Carolina.

C

In 2010, the Federal Trade Commission (FTC) filed an

administrative complaint charging the Board with violating §5 of the Federal Trade Commission Act, 38 Stat. 719, as amended, 15 U. S. C. §45. The FTC alleged that the Board's concerted action to exclude nondentists from the market for teeth whitening services in North Carolina constituted an anticompetitive and unfair method of competition. The Board moved to dismiss, alleging state-action immunity. An Administrative Law Judge (ALJ) denied the motion. On appeal, the FTC sustained the ALJ's ruling. It reasoned that, even assuming the Board had acted pursuant to a clearly articulated state policy to displace competition, the Board is a "public/private hybrid" that must be actively supervised by the State to claim immunity. App. to Pet. for Cert. 49a. The FTC further concluded the Board could not make that showing.

Following other proceedings not relevant here, the ALJ conducted a hearing on the merits and determined the Board had unreasonably restrained trade in violation of antitrust law. On appeal, the FTC again sustained the ALJ. The FTC rejected the Board's public safety justification, noting, *inter alia*, "a wealth of evidence . . . suggesting that non-dentist provided teeth whitening is a safe cosmetic procedure." *Id.,* at 123a.

The FTC ordered the Board to stop sending the cease-and-desist letters or other communications that stated nondentists may not offer teeth whitening services and products. It further ordered the Board to issue notices to all earlier recipients of the Board's cease-and-desist orders advising them of the Board's proper sphere of authority and saying, among other options, that the notice recipients had a right to seek declaratory rulings in state court.

On petition for review, the Court of Appeals for the Fourth Circuit affirmed the FTC in all respects. 717 F. 3d 359, 370 (2013). This Court granted certiorari. 571 U. S. ___ (2014).

II

Federal antitrust law is a central safeguard for the Nation's free market structures. In this regard it is "as important to the preservation of economic freedom and our free-enterprise system as the Bill of Rights is to the protection of our fundamental personal freedoms." *United States* v. *Topco Associates, Inc.*, 405 U. S. 596, 610 (1972). The antitrust laws declare a considered and decisive prohibition by the Federal Government of cartels, price fixing, and other combinations or practices that undermine the free market.

The Sherman Act, 26 Stat. 209, as amended, 15 U. S. C. §1 *et seq.*, serves to promote robust competition, which in turn empowers the States and provides their citizens with opportunities to pursue their own and the public's welfare. See *FTC* v. *Ticor Title Ins. Co.*, 504 U. S. 621, 632 (1992). The States, however, when acting in their respective realm, need not adhere in all contexts to a model of unfettered competition. While "the States regulate their economies in many ways not inconsistent with the antitrust laws," *id.,* at 635–636, in some spheres they impose restrictions on occupations, confer exclusive or shared rights to dominate a market, or otherwise limit competition to achieve public objectives. If every duly enacted state law or policy were required to conform to the mandates of the Sherman Act, thus promoting competition at the expense of other values a State may deem fundamental, federal antitrust law would impose an impermissible burden on the States' power to regulate. See *Exxon Corp.* v. *Governor of Maryland*, 437 U. S. 117, 133 (1978); see also Easterbrook, Antitrust and the Economics of Federalism, 26 J. Law & Econ. 23, 24 (1983).

For these reasons, the Court in *Parker* v. *Brown* interpreted the antitrust laws to confer immunity on anticompetitive conduct by the States when acting in their sovereign capacity. See 317 U. S., at 350–351. That ruling recognized Congress' purpose to respect the federal balance and to "embody in the Sherman Act the federalism principle that the States possess a significant measure of sovereignty under our Constitution." *Community Communications Co.* v. *Boulder*, 455 U. S. 40, 53 (1982). Since 1943, the Court has reaffirmed the importance of *Parker*'s central holding. See, *e.g., Ticor, supra,* at 632–637; *Hoover* v. *Ronwin*, 466 U. S. 558, 568 (1984); *Lafayette* v. *Louisiana Power & Light Co.*, 435 U. S. 389, 394–400 (1978).

III

In this case the Board argues its members were invested by North Carolina with the power of the State and that, as a result, the Board's actions are cloaked with *Parker* immunity. This argument fails, however. A nonsovereign actor controlled by active market participants—such as the Board—enjoys *Parker* immunity only if it satisfies two requirements: "first that 'the challenged restraint . . . be one clearly articulated and affirmatively expressed as state policy,' and second that 'the policy . . . be actively supervised by the State.'" *FTC* v. *Phoebe Putney Health System, Inc.,* 568 U. S. ___, ___ (2013) (slip op., at 7) (quoting *California Retail Liquor Dealers Assn.* v. *Midcal Aluminum, Inc.,* 445 U. S. 97, 105 (1980)). The parties have assumed that the clear articulation requirement is satisfied, and we do the same. While North Carolina prohibits the unauthorized practice of dentistry, however, its Act is silent on whether that broad prohibition covers teeth whitening. Here, the Board did not receive active supervision by the State when it interpreted the Act as addressing teeth whitening and when it enforced that policy by issuing cease-and-desist letters to nondentist teeth whiteners.

A

Although state-action immunity exists to avoid conflicts

between state sovereignty and the Nation's commitment to a policy of robust competition, *Parker* immunity is not unbounded. "[G]iven the fundamental national values of free enterprise and economic competition that are embodied in the federal antitrust laws, 'state action immunity is disfavored, much as are repeals by implication.'" *Phoebe Putney, supra,* at ___ (slip op., at 7) (quoting *Ticor, supra,* at 636).

An entity may not invoke *Parker* immunity unless the actions in question are an exercise of the State's sovereign power. See *Columbia* v. *Omni Outdoor Advertising, Inc.,* 499 U. S. 365, 374 (1991). State legislation and "decision[s] of a state supreme court, acting legislatively rather than judicially," will satisfy this standard, and "*ipso facto* are exempt from the operation of the antitrust laws" because they are an undoubted exercise of state sovereign authority. *Hoover, supra,* at 567–568.

But while the Sherman Act confers immunity on the States' own anticompetitive policies out of respect for federalism, it does not always confer immunity where, as here, a State delegates control over a market to a nonsovereign actor. See *Parker, supra,* at 351 ("[A] state does not give immunity to those who violate the Sherman Act by authorizing them to violate it, or by declaring that their action is lawful"). For purposes of *Parker,* a nonsovereign actor is one whose conduct does not automatically qualify as that of the sovereign State itself. See *Hoover, supra,* at 567–568. State agencies are not simply by their governmental character sovereign actors for purposes of state-action immunity. See *Goldfarb* v. *Virginia State Bar,* 421 U. S. 773, 791 (1975) ("The fact that the State Bar is a state agency for some limited purposes does not create an antitrust shield that allows it to foster anticompetitive practices for the benefit of its members"). Immunity for state agencies, therefore, requires more than a mere facade of state involvement, for it is necessary in light of

Parker's rationale to ensure the States accept political accountability for anticompetitive conduct they permit and control. See *Ticor*, 504 U. S., at 636.

Limits on state-action immunity are most essential when the State seeks to delegate its regulatory power to active market participants, for established ethical standards may blend with private anticompetitive motives in a way difficult even for market participants to discern. Dual allegiances are not always apparent to an actor. In consequence, active market participants cannot be allowed to regulate their own markets free from antitrust accountability. See *Midcal, supra*, at 106 ("The national policy in favor of competition cannot be thwarted by casting [a] gauzy cloak of state involvement over what is essentially a private price-fixing arrangement"). Indeed, prohibitions against anticompetitive self-regulation by active market participants are an axiom of federal antitrust policy. See, *e.g., Allied Tube & Conduit Corp.* v. *Indian Head, Inc.,* 486 U. S. 492, 501 (1988); *Hoover, supra*, at 584 (Stevens, J., dissenting) ("The risk that private regulation of market entry, prices, or output may be designed to confer monopoly profits on members of an industry at the expense of the consuming public has been the central concern of . . . our antitrust jurisprudence"); see also Elhauge, The Scope of Antitrust Process, 104 Harv. L. Rev. 667, 672 (1991). So it follows that, under *Parker* and the Supremacy Clause, the States' greater power to attain an end does not include the lesser power to negate the congressional judgment embodied in the Sherman Act through unsupervised delegations to active market participants. See Garland, Antitrust and State Action: Economic Efficiency and the Political Process, 96 Yale L. J. 486, 500 (1986).

Parker immunity requires that the anticompetitive conduct of nonsovereign actors, especially those authorized by the State to regulate their own profession, result from procedures that suffice to make it the State's own.

See *Goldfarb, supra*, at 790; see also 1A P. Areeda & H. Hovencamp, Antitrust Law ¶226, p. 180 (4th ed. 2013) (Areeda & Hovencamp). The question is not whether the challenged conduct is efficient, well-functioning, or wise. See *Ticor, supra*, at 634–635. Rather, it is "whether anti-competitive conduct engaged in by [nonsovereign actors] should be deemed state action and thus shielded from the antitrust laws." *Patrick* v. *Burget*, 486 U. S. 94, 100 (1988).

To answer this question, the Court applies the two-part test set forth in *California Retail Liquor Dealers Assn.* v. *Midcal Aluminum, Inc.*, 445 U. S. 97, a case arising from California's delegation of price-fixing authority to wine merchants. Under *Midcal*, "[a] state law or regulatory scheme cannot be the basis for antitrust immunity unless, first, the State has articulated a clear policy to allow the anticompetitive conduct, and second, the State provides active supervision of [the] anticompetitive conduct." *Ticor, supra*, at 631 (citing *Midcal, supra*, at 105).

Midcal's clear articulation requirement is satisfied "where the displacement of competition [is] the inherent, logical, or ordinary result of the exercise of authority delegated by the state legislature. In that scenario, the State must have foreseen and implicitly endorsed the anticompetitive effects as consistent with its policy goals." *Phoebe Putney*, 568 U. S., at ___ (slip op., at 11). The active supervision requirement demands, *inter alia*, "that state officials have and exercise power to review particular anticompetitive acts of private parties and disapprove those that fail to accord with state policy." *Patrick, supra*, U. S., at 101.

The two requirements set forth in *Midcal* provide a proper analytical framework to resolve the ultimate question whether an anticompetitive policy is indeed the policy of a State. The first requirement—clear articulation— rarely will achieve that goal by itself, for a policy may satisfy this test yet still be defined at so high a level of generality as to leave open critical questions about how and to what extent the market should be regulated. See *Ticor, supra,* at 636–637. Entities purporting to act under state authority might diverge from the State's considered definition of the public good. The resulting asymmetry between a state policy and its implementation can invite private self-dealing. The second *Midcal* requirement—active supervision—seeks to avoid this harm by requiring the State to review and approve interstitial policies made by the entity claiming immunity.

Midcal's supervision rule "stems from the recognition that '[w]here a private party is engaging in anticompetitive activity, there is a real danger that he is acting to further his own interests, rather than the governmental interests of the State.'" *Patrick, supra,* at 100. Concern about the private incentives of active market participants animates *Midcal*'s supervision mandate, which demands "realistic assurance that a private party's anticompetitive conduct promotes state policy, rather than merely the party's individual interests." *Patrick, supra,* at 101.

B

In determining whether anticompetitive policies and conduct are indeed the action of a State in its sovereign capacity, there are instances in which an actor can be excused from *Midcal*'s active supervision requirement. In *Hallie* v. *Eau Claire,* 471 U. S. 34, 45 (1985), the Court held municipalities are subject exclusively to *Midcal*'s "'clear articulation'" requirement. That rule, the Court observed, is consistent with the objective of ensuring that the policy at issue be one enacted by the State itself. *Hallie* explained that "[w]here the actor is a municipality, there is little or no danger that it is involved in a private price-fixing arrangement. The only real danger is that it will seek to further purely parochial public interests at the

expense of more overriding state goals." 471 U. S., at 47.
Hallie further observed that municipalities are electorally
accountable and lack the kind of private incentives charac-
teristic of active participants in the market. See *id.,* at 45,
n. 9. Critically, the municipality in *Hallie* exercised a
wide range of governmental powers across different economic spheres, substantially reducing the risk that it
would pursue private interests while regulating any single
field. See *ibid.* That *Hallie* excused municipalities from
Midcal's supervision rule for these reasons all but confirms the rule's applicability to actors controlled by active
market participants, who ordinarily have none of the
features justifying the narrow exception *Hallie* identified.
See 471 U. S., at 45.

Following *Goldfarb, Midcal,* and *Hallie,* which clarified
the conditions under which *Parker* immunity attaches to
the conduct of a nonsovereign actor, the Court in *Columbia* v. *Omni Outdoor Advertising, Inc.,* 499 U. S. 365,
addressed whether an otherwise immune entity could lose
immunity for conspiring with private parties. In *Omni,* an
aspiring billboard merchant argued that the city of Columbia, South Carolina, had violated the Sherman Act—
and forfeited its *Parker* immunity—by anticompetitively
conspiring with an established local company in passing
an ordinance restricting new billboard construction. 499
U. S., at 367–368. The Court disagreed, holding there is
no "conspiracy exception" to *Parker. Omni, supra,* at 374.

Omni, like the cases before it, recognized the importance
of drawing a line "relevant to the purposes of the Sherman
Act and of *Parker*: prohibiting the restriction of competition for private gain but permitting the restriction of
competition in the public interest." 499 U. S., at 378. In
the context of a municipal actor which, as in *Hallie,* exercised substantial governmental powers, *Omni* rejected a
conspiracy exception for "corruption" as vague and un-
workable, since "virtually all regulation benefits some

segments of the society and harms others" and may in that sense be seen as "'corrupt.'" 499 U. S., at 377. *Omni* also rejected subjective tests for corruption that would force a "deconstruction of the governmental process and probing of the official 'intent' that we have consistently sought to avoid." *Ibid.* Thus, whereas the cases preceding it addressed the preconditions of *Parker* immunity and engaged in an objective, *ex ante* inquiry into nonsovereign actors' structure and incentives, *Omni* made clear that recipients of immunity will not lose it on the basis of ad hoc and *ex post* questioning of their motives for making particular decisions.

Omni's holding makes it all the more necessary to ensure the conditions for granting immunity are met in the first place. The Court's two state-action immunity cases decided after *Omni* reinforce this point. In *Ticor* the Court affirmed that *Midcal*'s limits on delegation must ensure that "[a]ctual state involvement, not deference to private price-fixing arrangements under the general auspices of state law, is the precondition for immunity from federal law." 504 U. S., at 633. And in *Phoebe Putney* the Court observed that *Midcal*'s active supervision requirement, in particular, is an essential condition of state-action immunity when a nonsovereign actor has "an incentive to pursue [its] own self-interest under the guise of implementing state policies." 568 U. S., at ___ (slip op., at 8) (quoting *Hallie, supra,* at 46–47). The lesson is clear: *Midcal*'s active supervision test is an essential prerequisite of *Parker* immunity for any nonsovereign entity—public or private—controlled by active market participants.

C

The Board argues entities designated by the States as agencies are exempt from *Midcal*'s second requirement. That premise, however, cannot be reconciled with the Court's repeated conclusion that the need for supervision turns not on the formal designation given by States to regulators but on the risk that active market participants will pursue private interests in restraining trade.

State agencies controlled by active market participants, who possess singularly strong private interests, pose the very risk of self-dealing *Midcal*'s supervision requirement was created to address. See Areeda & Hovencamp ¶227, at 226. This conclusion does not question the good faith of state officers but rather is an assessment of the structural risk of market participants' confusing their own interests with the State's policy goals. See *Patrick*, 486 U. S., at 100–101.

The Court applied this reasoning to a state agency in *Goldfarb*. There the Court denied immunity to a state agency (the Virginia State Bar) controlled by market participants (lawyers) because the agency had "joined in what is essentially a private anticompetitive activity" for "the benefit of its members." 421 U. S., at 791, 792. This emphasis on the Bar's private interests explains why *Goldfarb*, though it predates *Midcal*, considered the lack of supervision by the Virginia Supreme Court to be a principal reason for denying immunity. See 421 U. S., at 791; see also *Hoover*, 466 U. S., at 569 (emphasizing lack of active supervision in *Goldfarb*); *Bates* v. *State Bar of Ariz.*, 433 U. S. 350, 361–362 (1977) (granting the Arizona Bar state-action immunity partly because its "rules are subject to pointed re-examination by the policymaker").

While *Hallie* stated "it is likely that active state supervision would also not be required" for agencies, 471 U. S., at 46, n. 10, the entity there, as was later the case in *Omni*, was an electorally accountable municipality with general regulatory powers and no private price-fixing agenda. In that and other respects the municipality was more like prototypical state agencies, not specialized boards dominated by active market participants. In important regards, agencies controlled by market participants are more similar to private trade associations vested by States with regulatory authority than to the agencies *Hallie* considered. And as the Court observed three years after *Hallie*, "[t]here is no doubt that the members of such associations often have economic incentives to restrain competition and that the product standards set by such associations have a serious potential for anticompetitive harm." *Allied Tube*, 486 U. S., at 500. For that reason, those associations must satisfy *Midcal*'s active supervision standard. See *Midcal*, 445 U. S., at 105–106.

The similarities between agencies controlled by active market participants and private trade associations are not eliminated simply because the former are given a formal designation by the State, vested with a measure of government power, and required to follow some procedural rules. See *Hallie*, *supra*, at 39 (rejecting "purely formalistic" analysis). *Parker* immunity does not derive from nomenclature alone. When a State empowers a group of active market participants to decide who can participate in its market, and on what terms, the need for supervision is manifest. See Areeda & Hovencamp ¶227, at 226. The Court holds today that a state board on which a controlling number of decisionmakers are active market participants in the occupation the board regulates must satisfy *Midcal*'s active supervision requirement in order to invoke state-action antitrust immunity.

D

The State argues that allowing this FTC order to stand will discourage dedicated citizens from serving on state agencies that regulate their own occupation. If this were so—and, for reasons to be noted, it need not be so—there would be some cause for concern. The States have a sovereign interest in structuring their governments, see *Gregory* v. *Ashcroft*, 501 U. S. 452, 460 (1991), and may conclude there are substantial benefits to staffing their agencies with experts in complex and technical subjects, see *Southern Motor Carriers Rate Conference, Inc.* v. *United States*, 471 U. S. 48, 64 (1985). There is, moreover, a long tradition of citizens esteemed by their professional colleagues devoting time, energy, and talent to enhancing the dignity of their calling.

Adherence to the idea that those who pursue a calling must embrace ethical standards that derive from a duty separate from the dictates of the State reaches back at least to the Hippocratic Oath. See generally S. Miles, The Hippocratic Oath and the Ethics of Medicine (2004). In the United States, there is a strong tradition of professional self-regulation, particularly with respect to the development of ethical rules. See generally R. Rotunda & J. Dzienkowski, Legal Ethics: The Lawyer's Deskbook on Professional Responsibility (2014); R. Baker, Before Bioethics: A History of American Medical Ethics From the Colonial Period to the Bioethics Revolution (2013). Dentists are no exception. The American Dental Association, for example, in an exercise of "the privilege and obligation of self-government," has "call[ed] upon dentists to follow high ethical standards," including "honesty, compassion, kindness, integrity, fairness and charity." American Dental Association, Principles of Ethics and Code of Professional Conduct 3–4 (2012). State laws and institutions are sustained by this tradition when they draw upon the expertise and commitment of professionals.

Today's holding is not inconsistent with that idea. The Board argues, however, that the potential for money damages will discourage members of regulated occupations from participating in state government. Cf. *Filarsky* v. *Delia*, 566 U. S. ___, ___ (2012) (slip op., at 12) (warning in the context of civil rights suits that the "the most talented candidates will decline public engagements if they do not receive the same immunity enjoyed by their public employee counterparts"). But this case, which does not

present a claim for money damages, does not offer occasion
to address the question whether agency officials, including
board members, may, under some circumstances, enjoy
immunity from damages liability. See *Goldfarb*, 421 U. S.,
at 792, n. 22; see also Brief for Respondent 56. And, of
course, the States may provide for the defense and indemnification of agency members in the event of litigation.

States, furthermore, can ensure *Parker* immunity is
available to agencies by adopting clear policies to displace
competition; and, if agencies controlled by active market
participants interpret or enforce those policies, the States
may provide active supervision. Precedent confirms this
principle. The Court has rejected the argument that it
would be unwise to apply the antitrust laws to professional
regulation absent compliance with the prerequisites for
invoking *Parker* immunity:

> "[Respondents] contend that effective peer review is
> essential to the provision of quality medical care and
> that any threat of antitrust liability will prevent phy-
> sicians from participating openly and actively in peer-
> review proceedings. This argument, however, essen-
> tially challenges the wisdom of applying the antitrust
> laws to the sphere of medical care, and as such is
> properly directed to the legislative branch. To the ex-
> tent that Congress has declined to exempt medical
> peer review from the reach of the antitrust laws, peer
> review is immune from antitrust scrutiny only if the
> State effectively has made this conduct its own." *Pat-
> rick*, 486 U. S. at 105–106 (footnote omitted).

The reasoning of *Patrick* v. *Burget* applies to this case
with full force, particularly in light of the risks licensing
boards dominated by market participants may pose to the
free market. See generally Edlin & Haw, Cartels by An-
other Name: Should Licensed Occupations Face Antitrust
Scrutiny? 162 U. Pa. L. Rev. 1093 (2014).

E

The Board does not contend in this Court that its anti-competitive conduct was actively supervised by the State or that it should receive *Parker* immunity on that basis.

By statute, North Carolina delegates control over the practice of dentistry to the Board. The Act, however, says nothing about teeth whitening, a practice that did not exist when it was passed. After receiving complaints from other dentists about the nondentists' cheaper services, the Board's dentist members—some of whom offered whitening services—acted to expel the dentists' competitors from the market. In so doing the Board relied upon cease-and-desist letters threatening criminal liability, rather than any of the powers at its disposal that would invoke oversight by a politically accountable official. With no active supervision by the State, North Carolina officials may well have been unaware that the Board had decided teeth whitening constitutes "the practice of dentistry" and sought to prohibit those who competed against dentists from participating in the teeth whitening market. Whether or not the Board exceeded its powers under North Carolina law, cf. *Omni*, 499 U. S., at 371–372, there is no evidence here of any decision by the State to initiate or concur with the Board's actions against the nondentists.

IV

The Board does not claim that the State exercised active, or indeed any, supervision over its conduct regarding nondentist teeth whiteners; and, as a result, no specific supervisory systems can be reviewed here. It suffices to note that the inquiry regarding active supervision is flexible and context-dependent. Active supervision need not entail day-to-day involvement in an agency's operations or micromanagement of its every decision. Rather, the question is whether the State's review mechanisms provide "realistic assurance" that a nonsovereign actor's anticompetitive conduct "promotes state policy, rather than merely the party's individual interests." *Patrick, supra,* at 100–101; see also *Ticor,* 504 U. S., at 639–640.

The Court has identified only a few constant requirements of active supervision: The supervisor must review the substance of the anticompetitive decision, not merely the procedures followed to produce it, see *Patrick,* 486 U. S., at 102–103; the supervisor must have the power to veto or modify particular decisions to ensure they accord with state policy, see *ibid.*; and the "mere potential for state supervision is not an adequate substitute for a decision by the State," *Ticor, supra,* at 638. Further, the state supervisor may not itself be an active market participant. In general, however, the adequacy of supervision otherwise will depend on all the circumstances of a case.

* * *

The Sherman Act protects competition while also respecting federalism. It does not authorize the States to abandon markets to the unsupervised control of active market participants, whether trade associations or hybrid agencies. If a State wants to rely on active market participants as regulators, it must provide active supervision if state-action immunity under *Parker* is to be invoked.

The judgment of the Court of Appeals for the Fourth Circuit is affirmed.

It is so ordered.

SUPREME COURT OF THE UNITED STATES

No. 13–534

NORTH CAROLINA STATE BOARD OF DENTAL EXAMINERS, PETITIONER *v.* FEDERAL TRADE COMMISSION

ON WRIT OF CERTIORARI TO THE UNITED STATES COURT OF APPEALS FOR THE FOURTH CIRCUIT

[February 25, 2015]

JUSTICE ALITO, with whom JUSTICE SCALIA and JUSTICE THOMAS join, dissenting.

The Court's decision in this case is based on a serious misunderstanding of the doctrine of state-action antitrust immunity that this Court recognized more than 60 years ago in *Parker* v. *Brown,* 317 U. S. 341 (1943). In *Parker,* the Court held that the Sherman Act does not prevent the States from continuing their age-old practice of enacting measures, such as licensing requirements, that are designed to protect the public health and welfare. *Id.,* at 352. The case now before us involves precisely this type of state regulation—North Carolina's laws governing the practice of dentistry, which are administered by the North Carolina Board of Dental Examiners (Board).

Today, however, the Court takes the unprecedented step of holding that *Parker* does not apply to the North Carolina Board because the Board is not structured in a way that merits a good-government seal of approval; that is, it is made up of practicing dentists who have a financial incentive to use the licensing laws to further the financial interests of the State's dentists. There is nothing new about the structure of the North Carolina Board. When the States first created medical and dental boards, well before the Sherman Act was enacted, they began to staff

them in this way.[1] Nor is there anything new about the
suspicion that the North Carolina Board—in attempting to
prevent persons other than dentists from performing
teeth-whitening procedures—was serving the interests of
dentists and not the public. Professional and occupational
licensing requirements have often been used in such a
way.[2] But that is not what *Parker* immunity is about.
Indeed, the very state program involved in that case was
unquestionably designed to benefit the regulated entities,
California raisin growers.

The question before us is not whether such programs
serve the public interest. The question, instead, is whether
this case is controlled by *Parker*, and the answer to that
question is clear. Under *Parker*, the Sherman Act (and
the Federal Trade Commission Act, see *FTC* v. *Ticor Title
Ins. Co.*, 504 U. S. 621, 635 (1992)) do not apply to state
agencies; the North Carolina Board of Dental Examiners
is a state agency; and that is the end of the matter. By
straying from this simple path, the Court has not only
distorted *Parker*; it has headed into a morass. Determining whether a state agency is structured in a way that
militates against regulatory capture is no easy task, and
there is reason to fear that today's decision will spawn
confusion. The Court has veered off course, and therefore
I cannot go along.

---

[1] S. White, History of Oral and Dental Science in America 197–
214 (1876) (detailing earliest American regulations of the practice of
dentistry).

[2] See, *e.g.*, R. Shrylock, Medical Licensing in America 29 (1967) (Shry-
lock) (detailing the deterioration of licensing regimes in the mid-19th
century, in part out of concerns about restraints on trade); Gellhorn,
The Abuse of Occupational Licensing, 44 U. Chi. L. Rev. 6 (1976);
Shepard, Licensing Restrictions and the Cost of Dental Care, 21 J. Law
& Econ. 137 (1978).

I

In order to understand the nature of *Parker* state-action immunity, it is helpful to recall the constitutional landscape in 1890 when the Sherman Act was enacted. At that time, this Court and Congress had an understanding of the scope of federal and state power that is very different from our understanding today. The States were understood to possess the exclusive authority to regulate "their purely internal affairs." *Leisy* v. *Hardin*, 135 U. S. 100, 122 (1890). In exercising their police power in this area, the States had long enacted measures, such as price controls and licensing requirements, that had the effect of restraining trade.[3]

The Sherman Act was enacted pursuant to Congress' power to regulate interstate commerce, and in passing the Act, Congress wanted to exercise that power "to the utmost extent." *United States* v. *South-Eastern Underwriters Assn.*, 322 U. S. 533, 558 (1944). But in 1890, the understanding of the commerce power was far more limited than it is today. See, *e.g., Kidd* v. *Pearson*, 128 U. S. 1, 17–18 (1888). As a result, the Act did not pose a threat to traditional state regulatory activity.

By 1943, when *Parker* was decided, however, the situation had changed dramatically. This Court had held that the commerce power permitted Congress to regulate even local activity if it "exerts a substantial economic effect on interstate commerce." *Wickard* v. *Filburn*, 317 U. S. 111, 125 (1942). This meant that Congress could regulate many of the matters that had once been thought to fall exclusively within the jurisdiction of the States. The new interpretation of the commerce power brought about an expansion of the reach of the Sherman Act. See *Hospital*

---

[3] See Handler, The Current Attack on the *Parker* v. *Brown* State Action Doctrine, 76 Colum. L. Rev. 1, 4–6 (1976) (collecting cases).

Building Co. v. *Trustees of Rex Hospital*, 425 U. S. 738, 743, n. 2 (1976) ("[D]ecisions by this Court have permitted the reach of the Sherman Act to expand along with expanding notions of congressional power"). And the expanded reach of the Sherman Act raised an important question. The Sherman Act does not expressly exempt States from its scope. Does that mean that the Act applies to the States and that it potentially outlaws many traditional state regulatory measures? The Court confronted that question in *Parker*.

In *Parker*, a raisin producer challenged the California Agricultural Prorate Act, an agricultural price support program. The California Act authorized the creation of an Agricultural Prorate Advisory Commission (Commission) to establish marketing plans for certain agricultural commodities within the State. 317 U. S., at 346–347. Raisins were among the regulated commodities, and so the Commission established a marketing program that governed many aspects of raisin sales, including the quality and quantity of raisins sold, the timing of sales, and the price at which raisins were sold. *Id.,* at 347–348. The *Parker* Court assumed that this program would have violated "the Sherman Act if it were organized and made effective solely by virtue of a contract, combination or conspiracy of private persons," and the Court also assumed that Congress could have prohibited a State from creating a program like California's if it had chosen to do so. *Id.,* at 350. Nevertheless, the Court concluded that the California program did not violate the Sherman Act because the Act did not circumscribe state regulatory power. *Id.,* at 351.

The Court's holding in *Parker* was not based on either the language of the Sherman Act or anything in the legislative history affirmatively showing that the Act was not meant to apply to the States. Instead, the Court reasoned that "[i]n a dual system of government in which, under the Constitution, the states are sovereign, save only as Congress may constitutionally subtract from their authority, an unexpressed purpose to nullify a state's control over its officers and agents is not lightly to be attributed to Congress." 317 U. S., at 351. For the Congress that enacted the Sherman Act in 1890, it would have been a truly radical and almost certainly futile step to attempt to prevent the States from exercising their traditional regulatory authority, and the *Parker* Court refused to assume that the Act was meant to have such an effect.

When the basis for the *Parker* state-action doctrine is understood, the Court's error in this case is plain. In 1890, the regulation of the practice of medicine and dentistry was regarded as falling squarely within the States' sovereign police power. By that time, many States had established medical and dental boards, often staffed by doctors or dentists,[4] and had given those boards the authority to confer and revoke licenses.[5] This was quintessential police power legislation, and although state laws were often challenged during that era under the doctrine of substantive due process, the licensing of medical professionals easily survived such assaults. Just one year before the enactment of the Sherman Act, in *Dent* v. *West Virginia*, 129 U. S. 114, 128 (1889), this Court rejected such a challenge to a state law requiring all physicians to obtain a certificate from the state board of health attesting to their qualifications. And in *Hawker* v. *New York*, 170 U. S. 189, 192 (1898), the Court reiterated that a law

---

[4] Shrylock 54–55; D. Johnson and H. Chaudry, Medical Licensing and Discipline in America 23–24 (2012).

[5] In *Hawker* v. *New York*, 170 U. S. 189 (1898), the Court cited state laws authorizing such boards to refuse or revoke medical licenses. *Id.*, at 191–193, n. 1. See also *Douglas* v. *Noble*, 261 U. S. 165, 166 (1923) ("In 1893 the legislature of Washington provided that only licensed persons should practice dentistry" and "vested the authority to license in a board of examiners, consisting of five practicing dentists").

specifying the qualifications to practice medicine was clearly a proper exercise of the police power. Thus, the North Carolina statutes establishing and specifying the powers of the State Board of Dental Examiners represent precisely the kind of state regulation that the *Parker* exemption was meant to immunize.

II

As noted above, the only question in this case is whether the North Carolina Board of Dental Examiners is really a state agency, and the answer to that question is clearly yes.

- The North Carolina Legislature determined that the practice of dentistry "affect[s] the public health, safety and welfare" of North Carolina's citizens and that therefore the profession should be "subject to regulation and control in the public interest" in order to ensure "that only qualified persons be permitted to practice dentistry in the State." N. C. Gen. Stat. Ann. §90–22(a) (2013).

- To further that end, the legislature created the North Carolina State Board of Dental Examiners "as the agency of the State for the regulation of the practice of dentistry in th[e] State." §90–22(b).

- The legislature specified the membership of the Board. §90–22(c). It defined the "practice of dentistry," §90–29(b), and it set out standards for licensing practitioners, §90–30. The legislature also set out standards under which the Board can initiate disciplinary proceedings against licensees who engage in certain improper acts. §90–41(a).

- The legislature empowered the Board to "maintain an action in the name of the State of North Carolina to perpetually enjoin any person from . . . unlawfully practicing dentistry." §90–40.1(a). It authorized the Board to conduct investigations and to hire legal counsel, and the legislature made any "notice or statement of charges against any licensee" a public record under state law. §§ 90–41(d)–(g).

- The legislature empowered the Board "to enact rules and regulations governing the practice of dentistry within the State," consistent with relevant statutes. §90–48. It has required that any such rules be included in the Board's annual report, which the Board must file with the North Carolina secretary of state, the state attorney general, and the legislature's Joint Regulatory Reform Committee. §93B–2. And if the Board fails to file the required report, state law demands that it be automatically suspended until it does so. *Ibid.*

As this regulatory regime demonstrates, North Carolina's Board of Dental Examiners is unmistakably a state agency created by the state legislature to serve a prescribed regulatory purpose and to do so using the State's power in cooperation with other arms of state government.

The Board is not a private or "nonsovereign" entity that the State of North Carolina has attempted to immunize from federal antitrust scrutiny. *Parker* made it clear that a State may not "'give immunity to those who violate the Sherman Act by authorizing them to violate it, or by declaring that their action is lawful.'" *Ante,* at 7 (quoting *Parker,* 317 U. S., at 351). When the *Parker* Court disapproved of any such attempt, it cited *Northern Securities Co.* v. *United States,* 193 U. S. 197 (1904), to show what it had in mind. In that case, the Court held that a State's act of chartering a corporation did not shield the corporation's monopolizing activities from federal antitrust law. *Id.,* at 344–345. Nothing similar is involved here. North Carolina did not authorize a private entity to enter into an anticompetitive arrangement; rather, North Carolina *created a state agency* and gave that agency the power to regulate a particular subject affecting public health and safety.

Nothing in *Parker* supports the type of inquiry that the Court now prescribes. The Court crafts a test under which state agencies that are "controlled by active market participants," *ante*, at 12, must demonstrate active state supervision in order to be immune from federal antitrust law. The Court thus treats these state agencies like private entities. But in *Parker*, the Court did not examine the structure of the California program to determine if it had been captured by private interests. If the Court had done so, the case would certainly have come out differently, because California conditioned its regulatory measures on the participation and approval of market actors in the relevant industry.

Establishing a prorate marketing plan under California's law first required the petition of at least 10 producers of the particular commodity. *Parker*, 317 U. S., at 346. If the Commission then agreed that a marketing plan was warranted, the Commission would "select a program committee *from among nominees chosen by the qualified producers.*" *Ibid.* (emphasis added). That committee would then formulate the proration marketing program, which the Commission could modify or approve. But even after Commission approval, the program became law (and then, automatically) only if it gained the approval of 65 percent of the relevant producers, representing at least 51 percent of the acreage of the regulated crop. *Id.*, at 347. This scheme gave decisive power to market participants. But despite these aspects of the California program, *Parker* held that California was acting as a "sovereign" when it "adopt[ed] and enforc[ed] the prorate program." *Id.*, at 352. This reasoning is irreconcilable with the Court's today.

                            III

The Court goes astray because it forgets the origin of the

Parker doctrine and is misdirected by subsequent cases that extended that doctrine (in certain circumstances) to private entities. The Court requires the North Carolina Board to satisfy the two-part test set out in *California Retail Liquor Dealers Assn.* v. *Midcal Aluminum, Inc.*, 445 U. S. 97 (1980), but the party claiming *Parker* immunity in that case was not a state agency but a private trade association. Such an entity is entitled to *Parker* immunity, *Midcal* held, only if the anticompetitive conduct at issue was both "'clearly articulated'" and "'actively supervised by the State itself.'" 445 U. S., at 105. Those requirements are needed where a State authorizes private parties to engage in anticompetitive conduct. They serve to identify those situations in which conduct *by private parties* can be regarded as the conduct of a State. But when the conduct in question is the conduct of a state agency, no such inquiry is required.

This case falls into the latter category, and therefore *Midcal* is inapposite. The North Carolina Board is not a private trade association. It is a state agency, created and empowered by the State to regulate an industry affecting public health. It would not exist if the State had not created it. And for purposes of *Parker*, its membership is irrelevant; what matters is that it is part of the government of the sovereign State of North Carolina.

Our decision in *Hallie* v. *Eau Claire*, 471 U. S. 34 (1985), which involved Sherman Act claims against a municipality, not a State agency, is similarly inapplicable. In *Hallie,* the plaintiff argued that the two-pronged *Midcal* test should be applied, but the Court disagreed. The Court acknowledged that municipalities "are not themselves sovereign." 471 U. S., at 38. But recognizing that a municipality is "an arm of the State," *id.*, at 45, the Court held that a municipality should be required to satisfy only the first prong of the *Midcal* test (requiring a clearly articulated state policy), 471 U. S., at 46. That municipalities are not sovereign was critical to our analysis in *Hallie*, and thus that decision has no application in a case, like this one, involving a state agency.

Here, however, the Court not only disregards the North Carolina Board's status as a full-fledged state agency; it treats the Board less favorably than a municipality. This is puzzling. States are sovereign, *Northern Ins. Co. of N. Y.* v. *Chatham County*, 547 U. S. 189, 193 (2006), and California's sovereignty provided the foundation for the decision in *Parker, supra,* at 352. Municipalities are not sovereign. *Jinks* v. *Richland County*, 538 U. S. 456, 466 (2003). And for this reason, federal law often treats municipalities differently from States. Compare *Will* v. *Michigan Dept. of State Police*, 491 U. S. 58, 71 (1989) ("[N]either a State nor its officials acting it their official capacities are 'persons' under [42 U. S. C.] §1983"), with *Monell* v. *City Dept. of Social Servs., New York*, 436 U. S. 658, 694 (1978) (municipalities liable under §1983 where "execution of a government's policy or custom . . . inflicts the injury").

The Court recognizes that municipalities, although not sovereign, nevertheless benefit from a more lenient standard for state-action immunity than private entities. Yet under the Court's approach, the North Carolina Board of Dental Examiners, a full-fledged state agency, is treated like a private actor and must demonstrate that the State actively supervises its actions.

The Court's analysis seems to be predicated on an assessment of the varying degrees to which a municipality and a state agency like the North Carolina Board are likely to be captured by private interests. But until today, *Parker* immunity was never conditioned on the proper use of state regulatory authority. On the contrary, in *Columbia* v. *Omni Outdoor Advertising, Inc.*, 499 U. S. 365 (1991), we refused to recognize an exception to *Parker* for cases in which it was shown that the defendants had engaged in a conspiracy or corruption or had acted in a way that was not in the public interest. *Id.,* at 374. The Sherman Act, we said, is not an anticorruption or good-government statute. 499 U. S., at 398. We were unwilling in *Omni* to rewrite *Parker* in order to reach the allegedly abusive behavior of city officials. 499 U. S., at 374–379. But that is essentially what the Court has done here.

III

Not only is the Court's decision inconsistent with the underlying theory of *Parker*; it will create practical problems and is likely to have far-reaching effects on the States' regulation of professions. As previously noted, state medical and dental boards have been staffed by practitioners since they were first created, and there are obvious advantages to this approach. It is reasonable for States to decide that the individuals best able to regulate technical professions are practitioners with expertise in those very professions. Staffing the State Board of Dental Examiners with certified public accountants would certainly lessen the risk of actions that place the well-being of dentists over those of the public, but this would also compromise the State's interest in sensibly regulating a technical profession in which lay people have little expertise.

As a result of today's decision, States may find it necessary to change the composition of medical, dental, and other boards, but it is not clear what sort of changes are needed to satisfy the test that the Court now adopts. The Court faults the structure of the North Carolina Board because "active market participants" constitute "a controlling number of [the] decisionmakers," *ante,* at 14, but this test raises many questions.

What is a "controlling number"? Is it a majority? And if so, why does the Court eschew that term? Or does the Court mean to leave open the possibility that something less than a majority might suffice in particular circum-

stances? Suppose that active market participants constitute a voting bloc that is generally able to get its way?
How about an obstructionist minority or an agency chair
empowered to set the agenda or veto regulations?

Who is an "active market participant"? If Board members withdraw from practice during a short term of service
but typically return to practice when their terms end, does
that mean that they are not active market participants
during their period of service?

What is the scope of the market in which a member may
not participate while serving on the board? Must the
market be relevant to the particular regulation being
challenged or merely to the jurisdiction of the entire agency?
Would the result in the present case be different if a
majority of the Board members, though practicing dentists, did not provide teeth whitening services? What if
they were orthodontists, periodontists, and the like? And
how much participation makes a person "active" in the
market?

The answers to these questions are not obvious, but the
States must predict the answers in order to make in-
formed choices about how to constitute their agencies.

I suppose that all this will be worked out by the lower
courts and the Federal Trade Commission (FTC), but the
Court's approach raises a more fundamental question, and
that is why the Court's inquiry should stop with an exam-
ination of the structure of a state licensing board. When
the Court asks whether market participants control the
North Carolina Board, the Court in essence is asking
whether this regulatory body has been captured by the
entities that it is supposed to regulate. Regulatory capture can occur in many ways.[6] So why ask only whether

---

[6] See, *e.g.*, R. Noll, Reforming Regulation 40–43, 46 (1971); J. Wilson,
The Politics of Regulation 357–394 (1980). Indeed, it has even been

the members of a board are active market participants? The answer may be that determining when regulatory capture has occurred is no simple task. That answer provides a reason for relieving courts from the obligation to make such determinations at all. It does not explain why it is appropriate for the Court to adopt the rather crude test for capture that constitutes the holding of today's decision.

IV

The Court has created a new standard for distinguishing between private and state actors for purposes of federal antitrust immunity. This new standard is not true to the *Parker* doctrine; it diminishes our traditional respect for federalism and state sovereignty; and it will be difficult to apply. I therefore respectfully dissent.

---

charged that the FTC, which brought this case, has been captured by entities over which it has jurisdiction. See E. Cox, "The Nader Report" on the Federal Trade Commission vii–xiv (1969); Posner, Federal Trade Commission, Chi. L. Rev. 47, 82–84 (1969).

www.ingramcontent.com/pod-product-compliance
Lightning Source LLC
Chambersburg PA
CBHW081540280526
45788CB00010B/3310